BASEBALL SHORT STORIES FOR KIDS

Diamond Adventures - Exciting and Entertaining Stories from the World of Baseball

Charlotte Gibbs

© Copyright 2023 - All rights reserved.

The content contained within this book may not be reproduced, duplicated or transmitted without direct written permission from the author or the publisher.

Under no circumstances will any blame or legal responsibility be held against the publisher, or author, for any damages, reparation, or monetary loss due to the information contained within this book, either directly or indirectly.

Legal Notice:

This book is copyright protected. It is only for personal use. You cannot amend, distribute, sell, use, quote or paraphrase any part, or the content within this book, without the consent of the author or publisher.

Disclaimer Notice:

Please note the information contained within this document is for educational and entertainment purposes only. All effort has been executed to present accurate, up to date, reliable, complete information. No warranties of any kind are declared or implied. Readers acknowledge that the author is not engaged in the rendering of legal, financial, medical or professional advice. The content within this book has been derived from various sources. Please consult a licensed professional before attempting any techniques outlined in this book.

By reading this document, the reader agrees that under no circumstances is the author responsible for any losses, direct or indirect, that are incurred as a result of the use of the information contained within this document, including, but not limited to, errors, omissions, or inaccuracies.

Table of Contents

Introduction 4

Chapter 1: A Head (ahead); A Home Run 7

Chapter 2: You're Out: 17-year-old Strikes
Out The Iron Horse & The Babe 11

Chapter 3: "Spike" Queen of Baseball 15

Chapter 4: Strange Times: A Bribe or A Straw Hat Shoulder Injury 19

Chapter 5: Jersey: Bill Veeck and His Zany Ideas 25

Chapter 6: Youppi! Running Back for the Grand Slam 29

Chapter 7: Bug Game 33

Chapter 8: Fans Toss Their Team an L 37

Chapter 9: Birds, The True Angels of the Outfield 41

Chapter 10: Say Hey "World"! The Catch: Willie Mays vs
Kevin Mitchell 45

Chapter 11: Lightning Crashes, Indians Win 49

Chapter 12: Holy Jinxes, Superstitions and Curses 53

Chapter 13: Switch-Hitting HRs for Baerga!
Picture (A Pitcher), A Grand Slam 57

Chapter 14: Will the real HR King, please rise? 63

Chapter 15: Fathers and Sons 67

Chapter 16: Steals Second, Goes Back to Steal First 73

Chapter 17: Cheaters Never (Really) Win 77

Chapter 18: Beautiful Steals 81

Chapter 19: Pitching Duels 85

Chapter 20: Greatest Pitchers 89

References 92

Introduction

Welcome! I have a question for you. Why do you think people have loved baseball for over one hundred years? It is a fantastic game mixed with superstition, super highs and crushing blows. That's why! Maybe you've also heard about the curses and the lockouts, and some serious stuff like players being told they'll never play the game they love again or some heroic moments, or those plays that leave you scratching your head and your mouth hanging open in shock?

All of those things mixed up together like a wonderful recipe make this game so magical and memorable.

Baseball, as we now know it, started in the mid-19th century in New York City. Originally called "rounders," it was played on a diamond-shaped field with four bases. Rules were added to make the game more exciting.

In the years to come, the fun game caught on, new teams and leagues were formed—and eventually, the American and National Leagues joined forces to become Major League Baseball (MLB).

Baseball has had its share of remarkable players. Take Babe Ruth, a Yankees legend; or Willie Mays, who played for the San Francisco Giants; and Hank Aaron, who played for the Milwaukee Braves and Atlanta Braves. Jackie Robinson made history in 1947. While not on the field, Bill Veeck's story was known for his inventiveness and, lucky for him, made him a lot of cash in the process! You have sports teams buying players to boost their playoff chances. It wouldn't be a thing without Bill!

Bugs and birds have shown love and helped the underdogs win big games; and you'll notice players using their heads or hands to entertain the fans with lightning-fast strikes, history-making strikeouts, pitching battles, silly mascots, and a backward home run. I hope you enjoy this trip around baseball as much as the fans who experienced the 'Shot Heard Round the World.' Anyway, it's time! Are you ready?

You may hear more about these players and some of their stories later in the book. Most of these stories have been around a while, but sometimes going back, way back, is pretty cool! Let's give it a shot, and stay tuned!

Chapter 1
A HEAD (AHEAD); A HOME RUN

You may have heard of Jose Canseco, the slugger. Or know that he has a twin brother? But I wonder, have you heard about the strange events of May 26, 1993?

It all started when Canseco and the Texas Rangers were playing the Cleveland Indians. At the plate, Carlos Martinez hit an easy fly ball that bounced off Canseco's head for a home run! I know, right?! A head, a home run! Confused? Let's go back and break this down.

There is a quote about April being a cruel month, but it had nothing on this May day. So that May day, Jose Canseco, a star that the Rangers desperately needed to shine as brightly as he did for the Oakland Athletics, was struggling. It's hard to imagine that this powerhouse player, known for his impressive power at the plate and sometimes unpredictable antics on the field, was having such a rough time finding his groove. But he was.

In 1993, Canseco was starting anew, and this stint as an outfielder for the Rangers was to help the team become playoff contenders. No one could've predicted the hilarity that occurred on that day.

Poor Canseco had the most unusual assist in baseball history.

So how did the famous play happen?

Indians' infielder Carlos Martinez was at the plate. He swung, connected, and sent the ball toward left field. That ball was totally catchable and most likely would not make it over the wall.

Canseco ran to the warning track and got under the ball, but... oh no! He couldn't catch the ball from that position! The ball took an unexpected bounce off the top of Canseco's head and sailed over the outfield fence for a home run!

His fourth of the year, Martinez was thrilled, I'm pretty sure as he trotted around the bases after his unexpected home run.

Canseco's teammate, David Hulse, couldn't stop laughing. The announcers couldn't keep it together, either. Canseco was stunned and shaking his stunned baseball-bounced-on head in disbelief. He wasn't sure what to do! At first, he tried to play it off, pretending that nothing had happened. Fair enough. But the replay of the incident quickly went viral (by viral, the play was repeatedly played over and over on all popular sports shows and was most discussed 'misplay of the day' on local radio stations). For weeks, people talked about this play!

What a stroke of luck for Martinez. It showed that even professional athletes could have random, silly, unexpected and funny moments on the field. Not to mention, extremely entertaining. Despite the embarrassment, Canseco eventually laughed it off and even made jokes about his bad luck. On Twitter, he said the play should've been a four-base error.

I guess the message here is not to forget to laugh at yourself and be positive, like Canseco was, even if he took a little while to get there! A few laughs go a long way to make an embarrassing moment not so bad.

Chapter 2
YOU'RE OUT! 17-YEAR-OLD STRIKES OUT THE IRON HORSE AND THE BABE

Jackie Mitchell was a professional baseball player that made history when she struck out Babe Ruth and Lou Gehrig, two of the greatest players ever, in an exhibition game in 1931. Born on August 29, 1913, in Chattanooga, Tennessee, she started playing baseball when she was young.

Mitchell's father introduced her to baseball early on; and as luck would have it, their next-door neighbor was the famous pitcher Dazzy Vance! He'd played professional baseball for twenty years and was inducted into the Hall of Fame. For seven consecutive seasons, Vance was the only player to lead in strikeouts.

Do you think Mitchell's playful energy and enthusiasm drew Vance in?

Maybe.

As they spent time together, Vance showed Jackie all the tricks of the trade, like how to make her breaking ball come alive in her hands moments before she hurled it through the air. Talk about a lucky girl!

Fast forward a few years, and Mitchell's unique sidearm delivery fascinated sports reporters. Her delivery enhanced her pitches' curve, speed, and velocity. Her best feature, though, was her control. Jackie had a knack for picking her spots; an explosive combination of fastballs and curveballs. Also, she could quickly read and sense a batter's weakness; her pitches landed exactly where she wanted. Many Chattanoogan newspaper stories of the time thought she was a sure bet to make it and to become the first woman to become a regular big-league pitcher. Go, girl!

And you know what, her chance did come. At seventeen, the Chattanooga Lookouts, a minor league team, inked Jackie to a contract after the team's manager saw her pitching skills. The Lookouts took on the mighty Yankees in an exhibition game on April 2, 1931.

In the sixth inning of the game, with the Yankees leading 6-2, they brought Jackie in to pitch. On deck were Babe Ruth and Lou Gehrig.

First up. The Bambino—one of Ruth's many nicknames!

Mitchell hurled her sinker.

First pitch, ball.

Ruth swung and missed the next two pitches.

Angrily, he asked the umpire to inspect the ball. The umpire threw a new one out to Mitchell.

Ruth struck out on the fourth pitch. He was livid and started yelling at the umpire. His teammates had to rush to the field to drag him away!

Next up. Buster or Hungry Lou. The Iron Horse himself.

Lou Gehrig.

But he struck out in three straight pitches.

Despite the pressure, Jackie had done it!

Picture the crowd's shocked silence before they went wild. Jackie became an instant sensation. I'm sure she got a standing ovation. Imagine the crowd losing their minds—they just witnessed history!

Unfortunately, that was the end of the game for Jackie. The next batter(s) got a walk or a double, and she was pulled out of the game. Jackie never played in a regular season game in the major leagues again, as women were not allowed play at that level back then. A shame, huh? But she continued to play in the minor leagues and barnstorming circuits for a few more years before retiring from baseball.

Jackie's legacy lives on as a trailblazer for women in baseball. Jackie took out two of the greatest players, but it wasn't long before everyone had forgotten all about it! It wasn't until the 1990s that an article about the game brought Mitchell's accomplishments back to public attention. And we're so glad they did!

Jackie shows us not to be afraid to be brave. To trust yourself and just go for it! That you can show others the way if you dare to be first.

for the Rangers was to help the team become playoff contenders. No one could've predicted the hilarity that occurred on that day.

Chapter 3
"SPIKE" QUEEN OF BASEBALL

Born and raised in Rhode Island, Lizzie Murphy nicknamed herself "Spike." She was passionate about sports and enjoyed skating, swimming, track, and hockey. Besides sports, Lizzie spoke French, enjoyed cooking, and played the violin. What an all-rounder!

Lizzie was proud to be the first female to play for All-Star teams in both the National and American Leagues; she was also the first female holdout, refusing to play without pay. We like her style!

Her gamble paid off. And led to a 25-year career touring all over New England and Canada, playing 90 + games a summer. Sadly, being a premiere athlete didn't pay well (or at all) back then, mainly when very few women played baseball (or any sport professionally); but she built a solid reputation as a first-base player who was also a decent hitter.

Murphy was actually a brilliant baseball player. Remember earlier when I mentioned she spoke French? One time when she was playing in a game in Quebec, Lizzie overheard the coach at first base setting up the steal signals. Little did he know Murphy could understand him.

Ha! She stayed quiet and quickly thought up a secret sign for her catcher. Her team tagged out five runners because of Lizzie's little secret strategy. Did I mention we like her style?!

Lizzie tended to bet on herself. She had to make extra money. Before custom-made jerseys were a thing, Lizzie had a specially made uniform with her name embroidered on the front and sold postcards featuring her wearing her custom-made uniform to make extra money.

On August 14, 1922, her most famous game was held at Fenway Park. The American League All-Stars and Boston Red Sox exhibition game was organized to fundraise for the family of player Tommy McCarthy. The proceeds went to his widow and daughters.

During the game, Lizzie started on first base, playing a few innings and having one at-bat against pitcher Allen Russell. She ended up grounding out to the shortstop before Doc Johnston took her place. Did you know she was the only player in the game who wasn't a regular major leaguer?

In 1935, Lizzie stopped playing baseball and moved to Warren, RI. Two years later, Lizzie was married. She enjoyed married life for a few years before setting on a new career path. Get this. Instead of returning to baseball, Lizzie supported herself and her mom in odd jobs like working in the mills, and then on oyster boats.

Decades later a few people tried to get her back into baseball. At one point, she was asked to join a Little League celebration, but she declined and said she didn't want to take part. Sometime later, when a group of friends wanted to throw a dinner to commemorate her achievements in the sport, Lizzie refused, insisting she didn't want to celebrate.

Although she had fond memories of her glory days, Lizzie didn't want to return to them. She was proud of what she had done and she was also happy to move on. People's priorities change and we need to respect their wishes of what they want to do with their lives.

Lizzie didn't cling to her past, and neither should we! She knew when it was time to let go and move on to something else. She lived entirely in the present, and that's really where happiness lives. Take advantage of the opportunities that could bring you joy in the future, and grab them, like a great ball catch!

Chapter 4
STRANGE TIMES - A BRIBE OR A SHOULDER INJURY

Let me tell you about Rube Waddell, a pitcher from the early 1900s who was known for his eccentric behavior both on and off the field—it's a crazy funny story! George Edward "Rube" Waddell was born in 1876 in Pennsylvania with a gift; his arm!

Let's begin with Rube's backstory.

Waddell was a super-talented baseball player who could throw a ball fast and easily strike out other players. He was almost as incredible as Christy Mathewson, another famous pitcher from around that time. When Waddell started playing for the Athletics in 1902, he was excellent, and nobody could hit his pitches. Rube was the best at striking out players (check out his stats) in 1902, 1903, and especially in 1904, when he broke a record by striking out 349 players! Wow! That record stood for a really long time until Sandy Koufax finally broke it 61 years later. In 1905, even though Waddell struck out fewer batters than he usually did, he managed a league-leading 287 Ks that year. He was so good that he won the American League pitching title three times! Waddell played for many teams, like the Pittsburgh Pirates and the Philadelphia Athletics.

But Rube was also known for his eccentric personality. He had a habit of chasing fire engines down the street - we're not quite sure why! But we like it! And he once famously left a game in the middle of an inning to chase after a passing fire truck! He also loved animals and was known to stop a game to pet a stray dog or feed a stray cat. We like that too!

One controversial aspect of Rube Waddell's career, while he was still playing and a century later, happened toward the end of the 1905 season that resulted in Waddell missing the World Series—a time when his team really needed him (and his ability to strike out hitters).

The story goes that Rube and a teammate were clowning around and being a bit rough (maybe it was nerves, or perhaps they were excited about how well the season was going). Anyway, on September 8, 1905, for whatever reason, Waddell tried to destroy a straw hat worn by Philadelphia Athletics teammate Andy Coakley at the train station in Providence, RI. (What's with Rhode Island (RI)? Huh? Is there baseball magic here, like that baseball movie with Heaven and Iowa?)

Jokes aside, Rube hurt his shoulder in the shenanigans causing him to miss most of the last month of the regular season and all of the World Series versus the New York Giants. Bet he regrets mucking about! Or maybe he was able to totally let it go like Lizzie can!

Biographies of Waddell and Connie Mack, his manager, have talked about this infamous event. Whether Waddell was injured as he claimed, or was bribed to fake an injury (rumours abound!) has remained at the core of the controversy. Most writers have taken a sympathetic view—they don't feel Waddell took a bribe or faked his injury. Stuff just happens when we clown around.

Now, here are some of my favorite stories about Rube in no particular order (some are verified, others are urban legends):

- Once, during a game, Rube noticed a fan eating a sandwich in the stands. He asked the fan if he could have a bite, and the fan obliged. Rube then walked off the field and sat in the stands with a fan, eating a sandwich and watching the game. I guess he was hungry!

- Rube would walk through the stands in his street clothes, changing into his uniform as he headed to the mound to play. Well, why not I say.

- Rube was also known for his love of fishing. He was spotted fishing in a nearby river during a game, still wearing his uniform. You read right, during a game! When the team manager found out, he had to send someone to get Rube and bring him back to the game. Gives a little more meaning to 'Gone Fishing!'

- Rube had a habit of disappearing for days, often reappearing in a different town. He once missed a game because he was off chasing a tornado. Fire trucks, tornados…

- Rube loved practical jokes. During one game, he convinced the opposing team's third baseman that a fly ball was a foul ball. I feel a little bad for that poor third-baseman.

Despite all of his antics, Rube was still a talented pitcher. And, I think it's safe to say that Waddell's antics would not have been tolerated by any other player because Rube was a famous pitcher that fans paid (and wanted) to see.

Sadly, Rube's career was over before it started. He leaves a legacy as one of baseball's wildest and most entertaining players. And that's the story of Rube Waddell! Too much fun, and too much trouble!

While having fun is important, so is focusing on the tasks and being committed to being present. Otherwise, you can let others down. I guess there's that fine line between having fun and remembering what's important. We think you can absolutely manage both!

Chapter 5
JERSEYS AND FINDING THE BIG GUNS–BILL VEECK AND HIS ZANY IDEAS

How do organizers fill a stadium when the fans have lost all hope for the season? Tricky indeed. Because seats need butts on them! Enter innovative Hall of Fame owner Bill Veeck. His plan was to use brain, brawn, size, and one-of-a-kind ideas to his advantage to wow the crowd. Here are some of his most popular ones:

First up—finding talent and changing the game for the better. Veeck recruited Larry Doby in 1947, making him one of the first African-American players in the American League. Veeck didn't stop there. He was hungry to win, and one year later, he hired the oldest rookie ever, 42-year-old Satchel Paige.

Paige was a legend in the other leagues, and along with Doby, they pushed the Cleveland Indians to capture the World Series in 1948. Success.

Next up—a little stopover. It's August 19, 1951. Veeck had another of his stunts up his sleeve. Did you hear about the man who popped out of a cake? You didn't? Don't worry, the fans in the crowd that day was familiar with the man who would be the only player to wear a fraction. Yes, a fraction, like in math! It was Eddie Gaedel! The St. Louis Browns brought in jersey number $\frac{1}{8}$ to pinch-hit. Gaedel was 3-foot-7; the shortest player to date to appear in an MLB game. I wonder if there were any talks of reducing the strike zone, to be fair. It wouldn't have mattered even if they did, because Veeck instructed Gaedel to take a walk. Four pitches later, $\frac{1}{8}$ walked, and his only major league appearance was over. Just like that. He was substituted for a pinch runner. Sadly, his contract was canceled (but he was allowed to keep his perfect on-base percentage).

One of Veeck's most incredibly imaginative goals was the "hire-a-player" idea—trading for stars from other teams. Another genius idea was introducing the tradition of singing "Take Me Out to the Ball Game" during the seventh-inning stretch. Fun times.

Bill Veeck was a famous baseball owner known for his creative ideas to make the game more exciting for fans, but he was also a clever businessman. He owned teams like the Cleveland Indians, St. Louis Browns, and the Chicago White Sox between 1946 and 1980. Unlike many team owners, Veeck didn't come from a wealthy family, but he still made a lot of money from his teams. In fact, in 1941, with only $19.37 in his pocket, he and his partner Charlie Grimm bought the Milwaukee baseball team, which was struggling financially.

Veeck turned the team around, winning three championships in five years. Then, he sold the team for an enormous profit of almost $305,000 in 1945. What a profit!

Trying new things is exciting because it helps us figure out who we are, even if things don't turn out how might have expected them to. We discover what we're made of, and more often than not, when we step out of our comfort zones, we really hit our strides! And remember, being brave is not being fearless, it's having some fear but trying your luck anyway. Bill shows us not to be afraid to think outside of the box. To try new ideas, even if they might sound a little crazy. You might just come out a winner like Bill.

Chapter 6
YOUPPI! RUNNING BACK FOR THE GRAND SLAM

O kay, so it is possible to hit a home run without a bat and a ball. Do you think I'm kidding? I'm not! There's a whole bunch of weird and wacky things you can do in baseball.

Let me tell you the story from the beginning, and take you back to September 2012, the day the home run was invisible. The Washington Nationals were facing the St. Louis Cardinals.

Stepping up to the plate in the first inning with the bases loaded, Michael Morse swung and hit the ball off the fence. After a bit of confusion, the original call was the ball bounced back into play, and Morse was tagged out because of the particular layout of Busch Stadium. After reviewing and realizing their error, the umpires changed the call to a home run. But everyone had to return to their original bases, and Morse stepped back into the batter's box.

He paused, someone "suggested" the invisible bat, and Morse swung at the imaginary pitch.

Yahoo News quotes Morse: "I was like, "What do you want me to do?'" Morse said. "So, I look over to the dugout, and everyone told me to swing, and I was like, "I'm not going to swing." But then Yadi (Yadier Molina) goes, "Swing! Swing!" I was like, "All right!" So, I swung. And it was pretty cool. It felt like spring training. It felt like a drill." (Big League Stew, 2012). Like, like, like, like!

"I guess I didn't have to [swing again] but if they had called me out, I never would have slept again. I felt like everyone was waiting for me to swing. I wasn't going to do it at all, but it was such a crazy moment, that I might as well have some fun with it." (Big League Stew, 2012). Yes, he might as well and provide some extra entertainment for the crowd and a little story for us!

The announcers, of course, also added to the fun. According to reports from USA Today: "There it goes. Right field, it is deep! SEE. YOU. LATER. Grand Slam, the Nationals are on top by four." (USA TODAY, 2012).

Washington had to go ten innings before they won the game 6-4, which meant they'd take the division if the Atlanta Braves failed to win. It was undoubtedly the strangest moment of that unbelievable season.

But the Nationals have a history of strange moments. Oh, yes they do.

Mascots are always a treat, whether from losing a foot race around the bases, missing a catch, a lopsided throw to home plate, or dancing on the dugout. Once upon a time, the Nationals used to be this scrappy team called the Montreal Expos (1969 - 2004). Their mascot was called Youppi! (French: Yippee!), and one night in 1989 vs. the Los Angeles Dodgers, Youppi! cemented its place in baseball's history books. The orange loveable, cuddly, and furry creature became the first and only mascot to ever be ejected from a Major League game!

Youppi! had two "strikes" against him already. Tommy Lasorda was a stern no-nonsense manager and he wasn't a fan of mascots! (He's also famous for an encounter with another mascot, the Phillie Phanatic). The game was a scoreless nail-biting pitcher's duel that was 22 innings long. It felt like two or three games had been played that night.

Can you imagine the frustration at that point, with the opposing team's mascot stomping on top of the dugout? It would feel like a pounding headache! I don't blame poor Youppi! He was tired, the game went to extra innings, and he just wanted to go home to bed. When the ump (umpire - cute word, hey?) noticed how wild things were between Lasorda and Youppi!, he did the only thing he could—he tossed the mascot!

The crowd booed and booed until finally, the ump (ha!)reversed his decision, but Youppi! had to promise to stay on the Expos' side. Sadly, the Expos ended up losing the game 1-0.

Being passionate is great. Better than bored and uninterested in life! And it can be contagious, motivating others to be passionate too. It's a lovely thing. But sometimes being too passionate can get you in trouble and be a bother to others. Another example of walking the fine line between two things, but if you always try your best to be considerate of others, you'll do just fine.

Chapter 7
THE. BUG. GAME

Oh gosh. Bugs. Pesky, little bugs. Pesky little black bugs that when poor Yankee's pitcher, Joba Chamberlain wiped the back of his neck and his hands were black with bugs! Ew! Joba was rattled; the bugs were also up his nose! Not to mention he was breathing them in. But the show must go on?! One walk and two wild pitches later, the Indians tied the game.

Was it a sign from the heavens?

Were the Yankees supposed to lose the American League Division Series (ALDS)? It seemed so.

Bugs. Took. Over. The. Game.

It all started when the winds of change began around the top of the eighth when the bugs started appearing. Maybe they just loved baseball and wanted to get close to the action? Maybe they were paid with yummy treats in order to distract the players? Maybe they had a taste for sweat?! Whatever the reason, they were there. And everywhere.

Batting third that inning was Doug Mientkiewicz. Mientkiewicz was overwhelmed by the bugs! I'm sure the players wanted to pretend all was cool and they couldn't possibly be affected by teeny bugs, not these big stars, but oh yes they were bugged. Big time. Mientkiewicz asked for multiple timeouts to swat and brush the bugs off. They were midges, by the way. Tiny little guys that could make a big impact.

Imagine how hard it was for Mientkiewicz to concentrate, and imagine the pitcher being upset because it seems like the timeouts were called to mess with his ability to concentrate. Oh, those nasty, bad bugs!

When the camera slowly zoomed in, those snowflakes transformed into their true (bug) selves; every inch of exposed skin was coated with bugs.

Chamberlain threw four straight balls to Grady Sizemore. Posada was next at bat. Oopsy, a wild pitch; Chamberlain signaled to the Yankees dugout. Torre sent someone out to the mound to help, bug spray in hand!

A battle of wits, of desperately hoping. Is it fair to hope? Will using the spray stop the bugs? To spray or not to spray? Who wants to breathe in all those chemicals? Breathe in bugs, or spray? Hmm.. Too much pressure. Why aren't the Indian players spraying themselves? Is it better to ignore the bugs?

Back to the game. Let's see what happens next.

After Chamberlain was sprayed, several other players drenched themselves with it too, hoping for relief. Mientkiewicz, however, refused as he figured it wouldn't do any good. The bug spray would've helped if he was getting bitten; he knew it wouldn't help if the bugs were only annoying and sticking to you.

And Mientkiewicz was right; the spray had the opposite effect, attracting even more bugs! Yep, as impossible as it may sound, even more bugs attached themselves to Chamberlain's sweaty skin. He looked irritated. Maybe the sweat caused some of the bug spray to get into his eyes (or when he wiped his eyes to get rid of the bugs).

At the top of the ninth, still no relief in sight, the number of bugs was becoming unbearable.

The Indians were used to these unwelcome visitors. And they used this knowledge to their advantage and did their best to ignore the bugs.

Would their focus be enough?

The Yankees kept fighting. First, an infield single, and a few plays later, the runner stole second. Now, it was time to bring that runner home—at bat was the season's league leader in RBIs to knock him in. The pitcher, in the zone, battling pitch after pitch, then on the ninth pitch of the at-bat, a 97 mph sinker inside the corner.

Inning over.

The bugs cleared after the ninth, and Cleveland won 2-1 in the 11th. It was an ALDS victory of epic proportions. It was enough to finish off the Yankees in Game 4, giving Cleveland their first MLB playoff series win in nearly a decade.

Chamberlain played off and on for a few years, unfortunately never reaching his full potential. Would things have been different if he didn't have to play the "Bug Game?" We'll never know.

What a shame. But it's the way the game works. Sometimes you can all right elements to be great, but things don't work out as planned. Sometimes you win, sometimes you lose. Fate is a journey, and it's the detours and often 'failings' that can actually hold the miracles. Finding blessings when things go well is easy! But when things don't go to plan, that's where you gotta dig deep and look for the silver linings in the cloud. And there's always a silver lining! I'm sure if you look back on moments in your life, there were times when things didn't go to plan but after some time, you think, "Oh, I'm glad it worked out that way!"

Chapter 8
FANS TOSS THEIR TEAM AN L

Y ou get a souvenir, a free item at a ballgame. You cherish that souvenir with all your heart, right? Not the case on August 10th, 1995. The fans gave back, in the very worst way!

As part of a Los Angeles Dodgers' celebration of past Rookie of the Year winners, 15,000 souvenir balls were given away. Awesome!

But it was in the seventh that something unexpected happened. The balls started flying from the stands. At first, only a few hundred landed, which delayed the game for around five minutes. The balls gave way to rain, off and on until the ninth. And yes, you guessed it; the balls started sailing onto the field again! One landed near St. Louis Cardinals right fielder John Mabry, who pretended he would throw it back at the fans but threw the stray ball into the bullpen. Did that stop the fans? Sadly, it didn't. Another ball was thrown toward Brian Jordan. Jordan looked at Mabry and shrugged. "What now?" they wondered.

Nothing happened for a little while. Play continued, but only for a short time. Six pitches later and there was a call no one liked on a 3-1 count to Raul Mondesi. Unfortunately, things got heated between Mondesi and Dodgers manager Tommy Lasorda. What happened next? You guessed it, the plate umpire (I mean, ump!) ejected Mondesi and Lasorda. Cooler heads couldn't prevail on the field (or in the stands), and soon the entire field was littered with souvenir baseballs! Whoever had the idea to give away the balls must have been shaking their head in regret! Eventually, the Cardinals players had enough and left the field.

And the poor ushers didn't have nets or a way to stop all the balls from being tossed in their direction! Finally, the fans stopped throwing the balls. Phew! But the poor grounds crew had to slowly fill up 19 to 21 buckets with the ball souvenirs. Aren't people supposed to want to keep souvenirs?!

About seven minutes later, the Cardinals returned to their positions on the field but... oh no! One fan decided to hold on to their ball, eagerly awaiting their chance. The fan launched the ball into the air, and it landed with a little thud in the outfield. Super rude, we think!

Can you picture the umps pointing to the fans in the stands? Then shouting, "You're out!" Well, maybe not that dramatic, but the umpire decided the game had to end via forfeit. The Cardinals were up 2-1, so technically, they were in the lead, but with the forfeit call, they officially won 9-0. (Why? It's a rule all forfeits become a victory of 9-0).

Tom Henke earned the save, and it was the last recorded forfeit in Major Leagues.

Check out some other (dis)honorable mentions, though not as memorable as August 10, 1995, because the umpires were more lenient.

- Now, back in the 90s, teams often naively passed fans' perfect toss-ables, and the fans couldn't control the urge to toss items onto the field.
- Fans throwing giveaway baseballs to celebrate home runs delayed a game twice during a 1990 game in San Diego. Oopsie!
- In 1993, as the club was in the middle of a controversial fire sale,

the Padres gave away baseballs at the first Saturday game of the year. About 100 ended up on the field. Insert eye roll!

- Also in 1993, in the middle of a weird game that involved ejections, fans in San Francisco discarded their giveaway "photo balls"—baseballs with pictures of players' faces on them.
- In 1995, Pirates fans threw hundreds of wooden pennant sticks that had been passed out before the game. It took almost 19 minutes to clear the field.
- How did the Expos fans celebrate Henry Rodriguez's home runs in 1996? Not with peanuts or crackerjacks, but by tossing candy ars.

Thankfully, all this rowdiness and disruption came to an end. By 1997, any item that could be thrown into the field during play had to be given away at the end of the game when the fans exited the ballpark.

So what do you think about all these souvenir and ball-throwing onto the field? We think that when we receive a gift, we should cherish it (or at least give it away to someone who will cherish it). It's not really nice or polite to throw things away carelessly, don't you think? Yes, I know you already know that. It's important to always be respectful; we don't like having the gifts that we give rejected, so we always try our best not to act in a way that can hurt others. If we don't want a gift, we can keep it and give it to someone else or to charity.

And disrupting the ball game - what do you think? We see how it's a bit of fun, and a thrill to throw something onto the field. But the main reason you're there is to watch a game and it's pretty unfair on the players, we think.

Chapter 9
BIRDS, THE TRUE ANGELS OF THE OUTFIELD

So during a game between the Atlanta Braves and the New York Mets, Dion James was hitting a ball when sadly, a pigeon got in its way. The bird and the ball collided, preventing the New York player from catching the ball and um, preventing the bird from carrying on its life! This resulted in instead of a routine pop-up for the Yankees' Kevin McReynolds, James gets a double. That bird took a sacrifice fly and jinxed the Yankees, unfortunately.

Dale Murphy was the next batter, and he hit a home run, bringing himself and James in. The Braves ended up winning! So that was that.

Next up, we go across the border to Canada.

Some time ago, there was a ballpark in Toronto called the Exhibition Stadium; this ballpark was a popular hangout spot for another type of bird, seagulls. It could have been due to all the leftover food, or maybe because of its position next to the lake. Whatever it was, they liked to hang out at the stadium. They may just like the baseball vibe!

With Lake Ontario being so close, the stadium was always cold at the start and end of baseball season. Brr! The Toronto Blue Jays' first game occurred in 1977. It was the only major league game ever played with a snow-covered field! It was so bad that the Jays had to borrow a Zamboni from the local hockey team, the Maple Leafs, to clear the field. That wasn't the only odd incident that year (sorry, I gotta mention another forfeit). The Baltimore Orioles manager took his team off the field on a windy September day that same year because he was worried about the bricks holding the bullpen tarps being dangerous. The Jays won without having to do anything—the only time since 1914 that a team voluntarily forfeited a game instead of the forfeit being called by the umpire.

Now, let's move on to that seagull incident back in 1983. In the bottom of the fifth inning, Winfield threw the ball he was using to warm up between innings back towards the dugout and hit... a seagull. Did Winfield do it on purpose, or was it an accident? Of course, it would have been an accident, he never figured he'd hit it! "I turned and whipped and threw the ball, you know, to the batboy and a bird happened to be there and it's unfortunate," he said.

So, Billy Martin, Winfield's manager, cracked a joke about the infamous incident. He said that's the first time Winfield's hit the cutoff man all year. All jokes aside, why did Winfield get in trouble? Who made the call? Was it really animal cruelty? What were they thinking?

No one hates the Yankees that much, right? Pat Gillick, the Blue Jays GM, later helped Winfield out. All was forgiven the following day. Well, the seagulls' family didn't care to comment about the incident, they had other plans. No one hates the White Sox, A's, Phillies or Braves that much, right?

Winfield got traded to the Blue Jays in '91, and it was a blessing in disguise as he turned out to be key in helping them win their first World Series. The Blue Jays became the only team outside the United States to win a World Series (twice—the Jays also won the '93 World Series!).

Imagine if those birds weren't around to guide the ball (and the player) in the right direction. A win is a win, especially if you can make history. Or should I say that even when things are hard, you never know how things will turn out later? Unexpected things are bound to occur in life. In fact, they will and we can't avoid them. We need to look at the big picture and know that someone good is around the corner, and everything will be okay. So, keep the faith, and don't give up!

Chapter 10
SAY HEY "WORLD"! THE CATCH - WILLIE MAYS VS KEVIN MITCHELL

So, here they are; those famous CATCHES! First, the more iconic and well-known Wille Mays, the Say Hey Kid!

Kids worldwide have tried to imitate the Willie Mays basket catch from sandlot games to Little League fields for decades! What makes 'The Catch' so mythical is that his coach had faith in him and allowed him to use this method of catching the ball. Mays said that he could use the basket catch, but he was warned that he had better not miss the ball—and as luck would have it, Mays never really did (well, he might have missed a ball, maybe two). Did you know the Hall of Famer perfected the basket catch while serving two years in the Army? Talk about making the most of your time!

How did he know to go for it?

When the ball finally settled inside the Say Hey Kid's glove, there wasn't much anybody could say. If you go back and watch the footage, you'll see the shocked fans. They couldn't have known it then, but they'd just witnessed what's still known as the most incredible defensive play ever! Jack Brickhouse said it was an "optical illusion," but it sure was legit. This play is so important in baseball history, that it's just called "The Catch."

To hear Willie Mays tell it, you'd think this was just another regular, unimportant, routine fly ball grab, not a catch in the eighth inning of a tied Game 1 of the 1954 World Series. Mays shrugged off the idea that the catch was challenging. To him, it was an easy one.

It's hard to believe that the catch wasn't even the most impressive part of "The Catch" for Mays! What was the most memorable part was the throw. Here's why: runners were on first and second. It was a shoo-in that if the ball fell, at least two or three runs would score. Larry Doby was on second base and noticed Mays had a shot at running it down. He retreated to second, thinking he might take two bases on a tag up because of the layout of the ballpark. No such luck, as Mays makes the basket catch and turns and fires the ball into second base in one motion, his hat flying off his head as he spins around to throw the ball to the cutoff man. Doby only made it to third, and the other runner was stuck at first.

Because of Mays, the San Francisco Giants would make it out of the inning, get a walk-off in the 10th, and eventually win the World Series.

Now, it's time for the top of the "World!" That's a sweet nickname! Peter Golenbock's book Amazin' tells how Gary Carter nicknamed Kevin Mitchell "World" for his incredible infield and outfield abilities.

Imagine getting a call from a shocked Willie Mays after you made a super catch. Mitchell reminisces about Mays asking him how he pulled it off since that was not what Mays had taught him.

When Mitchell sprinted into the dugout following the third out of the inning, his utterly stunned teammates could only greet him with speechlessness. Everyone else was astonished, too. You get it, E-V-E-R-Y-O-N-E! I mean, everyone; players, spectators, and announcers were all shocked.

Here's the play!

Ozzie Smith hit a fly ball down the left-field line that was heading into foul territory. Mitchell, playing shallow, sprinted over, alternating looks at the ball and calculating how much more space he had before the wall. As the ball dipped, Mitchell suddenly realized it was going over his head. Mitchell overran the ball, and because Smith was a left-handed hitter, the ball was also trailing away from Mitchell. He knew he couldn't get his glove hand over to catch the ball. Instincts took over, and barehanded, Mitchell reached up and grabbed the ball mere seconds before bumping into the wall.

Mitchell went above and beyond in 1989—his best season and one of the best in Giants' history.

We can be taught many things and given much advice from people who know their stuff. And we are wise to listen and learn from those who are in the know. But it's also super important to trust your own instinct, and use your wisdom to pick the best solutions for you; usually, they are the simplest and first to come to mind. This is no time for overthinking. Just go for it!

Chapter 11
LIGHTNING CRASHES, INDIANS WIN

O h, poor Ray Caldwell. Well, maybe not—an angel opened its eyes; it had a feeling that this (lightning) strike would lead the Indians to victory.

As soon as Cadwell signed up for a semi-pro team at 20 years old, Caldwell's stock rose as he threw with his right hand and hit with his left. By 1914, Caldwell had finally figured out how to use his powers effectively. For New York, he had a record of 18-9 with a 1.94 ERA and was considered a rising star destined to become a legend in the years to come. Grantland Rice, a famous sportswriter of the time, believed that Caldwell had the potential to be as great as other popular pitchers of the era like "Big Six" Christy Mathewson or "The Big Train" Walter Johnson. And in fact, Washington Senators toyed with the idea of trading Johnson for Caldwell when both were in their prime. Still, the American League president at the time warned the team it was a dangerous move because Caldwell had too much potential.

Ray Caldwell was a baseball pitcher who played for several teams in the early 1900s, including the New York Highlanders/Yankees,

Boston Red Sox, and Cleveland Indians. Caldwell was known for his fastball, curveball, and spitball (a type of pitch no longer used today). He had a successful start to his career with the New York Highlanders. He even threw at least 53 consecutive scoreless innings, but his team's poor run support led to a losing record—he went 32-38 in his first few years with the team. Even though Caldwell was very talented, his issues off the field, unfortunately, overshadowed his abilities on the field, and he bounced around to a few other teams, like Boston. When he signed with Boston in 1919, he went 7-4 with a 3.96 ERA.

Now, guess whom he bunked with on those road trips? An up-and-coming 24-year-old superstar who also became known for misbehaving, Babe Ruth. Only a short time afterward, Boston realized that the pairing was a huge mistake and cut Caldwell in early August.

In August 1919, Cleveland's player/manager, Tris Speaker, signed Caldwell. Caldwell started for the Indians on August 24, 1919. That August day started off well. He was pitching a shutout against the Philadelphia Athletics.

Still, lousy weather was brewing. You could also feel the charge in the air, and before long, the rain started pouring down, and soon dark clouds began taking over the sky. Knowing the lake-effect weather could change at any moment, the Cleveland players kept their positions hoping to get the last three outs as quickly as possible to end the game.

So far, so good.

Caldwell had two outs and needed one more to win the game, but then lightning crashed into the ground. A bolt struck him on the mound! The angels opened their eyes, a silence fell over the crowd, everyone was hoping that Caldwell was okay.

His teammates rushed to his aid, but held off when the first person to touch him was also shocked! What an intense drama that was unfolding before the spectator's eyes! Thankfully, Caldwell eventually regained consciousness and insisted on finishing the game. What a legend! Instead of letting his teammates take him to the hospital, he insisted on finishing the game and getting the last out.

Caldwell winds up and throws, and the batter hits a hard ground ball to the third baseman Willie Gardner, who bobbles it a bit before knocking it down and firing it to first to get the batter out. To the shock and awe of the spectators and players alike, Ray Caldwell (and his guardian angels), boosted the Indians to a victory, a complete game win in the most influential game of his life!

Caldwell's brush with electricity has been talked about a lot, and for a bit, it helped his career. Not that he'd have wished it to happen, but it did have its silver lining! He remained in Cleveland and was part of the team when they won the World Series in 1920.

Caldwell was very lucky that he was not seriously injured. If you're ever outside and the weather takes a turn, or if dark clouds are approaching, it's always better to be safe than sorry. So stop playing, get under some shelter and take up the game later, it's not going anywhere!

Chapter 12
HOLY JINXES, SUPERSTITIONS AND CURSES

If you had to choose, would prefer sports or art? (I know your answer, the art of sport!) I'm guessing though if you're read this far into this book, you're a bit of a sports fan. Am I right? But you weren't the Red Sox owner, Harry Frazee.

He was the owner of the legendary Red Sox, who won five of the first 15 World Series titles in Major League history. So, he knew he could make a lot of money by trading Babe Ruth, known as Bambino.

Frazee was a theatrical producer/director who, oddly enough, came to Boston from NYC—already in debt from his 1916 purchase of the team and needing cash to fund a play that ended up being a Broadway smash. Struggling with money troubles, Frazee agreed to let the Yankees take Ruth for the impressive sum of $100,000 on December 26th, 1916.

That's when the fortunes of the two teams swung dramatically. The Yankees became a powerhouse legacy team, winning title after title. At the same time, the Red Sox and its fans weathered the Bambino Curse, for that's what they called this losing streak after losing Babe Ruth.

To kill the curse, Red Sox fans spray painted a road sign "Reverse Curve" into "Reverse the Curse," searched for Ruth's piano, alleged to have been thrown into a pond outside Boston after a rowdy party in 1918, and even staged an exorcism outside Fenway Park!

The team failed to make it to the World Series four times in nearly a hundred years. Would you believe they lost three series in game seven?

It was only a victorious game on the field that could break the curse, which happened at last in 2004 when the Red Sox and Yankees met. Did you know the Yankees went on to win four World Series championships with Ruth?

In this AL Championship Series against the Yankees, Boston, who had fallen behind three games to none in the best-of-seven series, miraculously came from behind to clinch the series—the first team in history to storm back from such a deficit.

After 86 years, the Red Sox finally swept the St. Louis Cardinals in the World Series to take their first championship. Edgar Renteria made the last out of that series, wearing jersey number three (that's Ruth's number! Amazing, right?)

Next up. Talk to your parents (or grandparents) about how awesome it was to buy a magazine to take the cover (or a poster) and stick it on your wall. Back then, having a physical "NFT" earned you bragging rights, and it was easy to buy a frame to protect your treasure, too; it didn't take as much work as card collecting or building Lego towns (or spending hours and days learning the tricks to harvesting the best wood for your Minecraft palace!).

For the fans, waiting for their favorite player to be on the cover of Sports Illustrated (SI) was exciting! For the player (or team), it was a curse.

One of the first "victims of the curse" was Eddie Mathews, who played with the Braves; he broke his hand one week after SI released the issue!

Other notable mentions:

- 1987: Indians' Joe Carter and Cory Snyder headline the 1987 MLB preview in April. Cleveland ended the season at 61–101.
- 2010: At the start of the 2010 season, the April 27 SI cover showcased the Yankees' Derek Jeter, Mariano Rivera, Andy Pettitte, and Jorge Posada. A week later, Rivera, Pettitte, and Posada suffered injuries. Jeter was fine but had one of his weakest years, hitting just .270 with 10 home runs.
- 2011: As the World Series was about to begin, the Texas Rangers' Nelson Cruz was featured on the SI magazine cover on October 24, 2011. But the Rangers couldn't capitalize and lost the Series. At two points in Game 6, they were only one strike away from becoming the Series Champions.
- 2012: Albert Pujols was Sports Illustrated's baseball preview cover on March 26, 2012. The photo caption boasted the great slugger had a new lease on life with the Angels. It took Pujols 28 games and 111 at-bats with the Angels before he achieved a home run on May 6, 2012. Pujols had hit 445 career home runs before 2012, and he tied Ruth and Reggie Jackson for most home runs in a World Series game.

Sometimes having a lucky charm can be all the assurance you need to succeed. Players wear crosses on their necklaces for religious reasons or keep a favorite picture in their lockers. However; it's important to remember that while faith is important, and wanting a little luck on your side is only natural, only hard work and practice makes perfect!

Chapter 13
SWITCH-HITTING HRs FOR BAERGA! PICTURE (A PITCHER), A GRAND SLAM

Carlos Baerga. Switch-hitting home runs (HRs) in the same inning. The first time ever! Imagine the lucky fans that witnessed this historic event! A home run; special indeed, and then to have the player come back up later that inning to homer again; divine!

That HR-pop, you know the sound I mean. You can almost hear it; it happens just before the ball pops off the bat, then that moment of silence as you take in the swing, and watch the ball sail outta the park!

On April 8, 1993, the temperature remained comfortable, reaching 71 degrees. But the intensity of the game outshone the beauty of the day. Cleveland got off to a good start, with two in the first and three in the third. Carlos Baerga contributed with a double and a single, plus two runs. The Indians led 6-2 at the start of the seventh because of his early production, but in the top half of the inning, the Yankees got back into the game by scoring three runs.

A pinch-hitter led off the bottom half of the seventh, and finally, on the seventh pitch, he singled to right field. Carlos Baerga advanced to the batter's box on the right side to face lefty relief pitcher Steve Howe. Baerga put up a good fight against Howe, taking him all the way to a full count until Howe threw an inside fastball which Baerga connected with, smashing it over the left-center field wall with a strong swing.

The score moved up to 10-5. The Yankees brought in righty Steve Farr to halt the damage. He got two batters out in a hurry before his fastball went astray. Lofton hit a single that allowed another runner to come home. On his second turn up to bat in the inning, Espinoza hit a three-run homer to clear the bases. Baerga stepped into the box for the second time in the inning, this time from the left. The first pitch was a ball. So many things happened in that inning; tensions were mounting, and runs continued coming in. On a 2-0 count, Baerga blasted a high fastball to the empty bleachers in right-center field— punctuating an eight-hit, nine-run seventh frame that propelled the Indians to a 15-5 victory.

Baerga ran the bases almost nonchalantly, unknowingly; he didn't realize he had made history until he arrived back at the dugout. Baerga glanced at the scoreboard and realized he was the first ballplayer in history to hit an HR from both sides of the plate in the same inning. What a moment!

The fans wouldn't stop applauding, so Baerga came out of the dugout to show his gratitude. He was timid, still not quite believing what he'd accomplished. Baerga was asked to give up his uniform, cap, and the home run baseballs so they could be enshrined into Cooperstown. Oh, and the game ended with an Indians victory.

Next in home run magic, we're going to go to a beautiful July day in 1966. The Atlanta Braves played the San Francisco Giants at Candlestick Park. Tony Cloninger, a 25-year-old pitcher, made history. Stick around. I'll explain it to you soon.

The game started with the Braves taking a seven-run lead before Cloninger took the mound in the bottom of the first. The first Giants batter, Felipe Alou, popped out to second, and then Mack Jones singled. Hank Aaron forced Jones to second, and then Rico Carty singled to right field, followed by Joe Torre's deep center field home run, making it 3-0. Frank Bolling and Woody Woodward each singled, and Giants pitcher Joe Gibbon was replaced by Bob Priddy. Priddy walked Denis Menke to face Cloninger, who worked Priddy to a full count before hitting a grand slam, making it 7-0. Alou grounded out, which ended the inning.

Carty hit a home run in the second inning, making it 8-0. Willie McCovey struck out, and the Giants replaced him with Dick Dietz to catch, and Tom Haller moved to first base. Ray Sadecki became the third Giants pitcher in the third inning. Cloninger hit his second grand slam in the fourth inning, making it 13-0. Atlanta scored five runs on two hits, two walks, and two errors.

Cloninger's two grand slams came with two outs and were set up by Menke's walks to load the bases. He became the first National League player and major-league pitcher to hit two grand slams in a single game. Cloninger's performance helped the Braves win the game 17-3.

Tony Cloninger's incredible feat of hitting two grand slams in one game helped the Braves beat the Giants. Cloninger's performance is iconic. It was an extraordinary deed never done by any National Leaguer or major-league pitcher.

Having a unique skill that's a bit different to everyone else, like switch-hitting or writing left-handed may feel like something to be ashamed of. But hey, your unique qualities can be called upon when times are rough! And anyway, it's great to be unique! Imagine Cloninger helping keep his team in the game on the mound and at the plate.

Chapter 14
WILL THE REAL HR KING, PLEASE RISE?

Babe Ruth is one of baseball's earliest and most iconic home run hitters. Ruth was a larger-than-life figure who played for the New York Yankees in the 1920s and 1930s. Throughout his career, Ruth hit 714 home runs; he was known for his incredible power and ability to hit towering home runs that seemed to defy gravity.

In the 1960s and 1970s, a Japanese player named Sadaharu Oh dominated the baseball game in Japan. Oh played for the Yomiuri Giants and was known for his unique batting stance, which involved holding the bat high above his head. For his career, Oh hit a staggering 868 home runs, a record that stood for many years. Baseball is super popular in Japan, by the way!

Sadaharu Oh's record of 868 home runs is undoubtedly an impressive feat. Still, it is important to note that he achieved this record in the Japanese Professional Baseball League, not Major League Baseball (MLB) in the United States.

While Oh's home run record is recognized in Japan and is a testament to his incredible talent as a baseball player, it is not officially recognized by MLB. This is because the two leagues have different rules, regulations, and levels of competition, making it difficult to compare records between the two.

It's worth noting that players from Japan have succeeded in MLB, including Ichiro Suzuki, Shohei Ohtani, and Hideki Matsui, among others. These players have significantly helped the league bridge the gap between baseball in Japan and the United States.

So, until that gap is merged, Barry Bonds holds the MLB career home run record with 762. He surpassed Hank Aaron's 755 on August 7, 2007. Coming in third is Babe Ruth, who was the leader until Aaron broke Ruth's record in 1974. Rounding out the top contenders are Albert Pujols (703), Alex Rodriguez (696), Willie Mays (660), Ken Griffey, Jr. (630), Jim Thome (612), and Sammy Sosa (609).

Willie Mays was a legendary all-rounder known for his incredible athleticism and power-hitting. Mays knocked out 660 dingers in his career, and many people regard him as one of baseball's top all-around players. Mickey Mantle was another iconic home run hitter who played for the New York Yankees in the 1950s and 1960s. Mantle hit 536 home runs for his career and was known for his powerful left-handed swing.

In the 1990s and 2000s, several players, including Sammy Sosa, Mark McGwire, and Alex Rodriguez, were known for their home run-hitting abilities. Sosa and McGwire were involved in a home run race in 1998 that captivated the nation. Both players hit over 60 home runs that season, with McGwire coming out on top with 70! Alex Rodriguez, also known as A-Rod, hit 696 home runs for his career and won three MVP awards.

In recent years, players like Giancarlo Stanton and Aaron Judge have been making waves with their home run abilities. Stanton hit 59 home runs in 2017, while Judge hit 52. Both players are known for their incredible power and their ability to hit the ball to all parts of the field.

So how about that? Did you enjoy reading about all those amazing home-run kings? I certainly enjoyed writing about it. To see different people from different backgrounds and life experiences all contribute to the game by crushing a ball out of a park. Imagine all the little boys and girls who were influenced and inspired by these legends, and went on to achieve their own dreams because they saw something familiar in these players. You can inspire those around you, too, at school or with your family, and be the change you want to see. How do you do that? By just being yourself and showing your own unique colors and skills. Easy!

Chapter 15
FATHERS AND SONS

Stottlemyre, Griffey, Bonds, Alou, Guerrero, Alomar, Fielder, Gwynn, Bichette. Who is the best father-son duo in baseball? And who knew so many fathers and sons played in the Majors? (There's even a grandson-grandfather duo; Yastrezemski). There are many more duos, but not enough time to mention them all.

Baseball has long celebrated the bond between fathers and sons. The following players have excelled on the field. Here are my top picks as the greatest father-son duos in baseball history:

1. Bobby Bonds and Barry Bonds

Bobby Bonds was a superstar outfielder in the 1960s and 1970s, known for his speed, power, and versatility. He played for several teams, including the San Francisco Giants; Bobby Bonds was a three-time All-Star and won three Gold Gloves. His son, Barry Bonds, happily followed in his father's footsteps. This duo has batted out over 300 home runs and stole over 400 bases between them! Barry Bonds is the all-time leader in walks, intentional walks, and home runs. He won seven National League MVP awards during his career. He also holds the record for most home runs in a single season with 73.

2. Ken Griffey Sr. and Ken Griffey Jr.

Ken Griffey Sr. was a two-time All-Star outfielder who played for several teams, including the Cincinnati Reds, where he won two World Series championships. He was known for his clutch hitting and leadership on the field. His son, Ken Griffey Jr., was one of the most exciting players in baseball history. He was a 13-time All-Star and won 10 Gold Gloves during his career. He also hit 630 home runs, which ranks sixth on the all-time list. This duo played together for the 1990-91 Mariners and were famous for hitting back-to-back homers against the Angels on Sept. 14, 1990. How cool~ Griffey Sr. was ending a 19-year career with three All-Star games and two World Series victories with the Reds. While Griffey Jr. was at the beginning of his career, he later breezed into Cooperstown on the first ballot in 2016.

3. Vladimir Guerrero and Vladimir Guerrero Jr.

Vlad Jr. and his father are already on their way to becoming one of the most notable father-son pairing in baseball history. Vladdy's gunning for his dad's Hall of Fame numbers. In June 2022, the Blue Jays star took the field for his 403rd game, where he sent his 87th home run out of the park. Astonishingly, Vladdy "matched" his father, who, less than three decades ago, was an icon of the Montreal Expos, swiftly becoming one of the finest players in their franchise's history—in his initial 403 games, Vlad Sr. hit 87 long balls, too.

4. Felipe Alou and Moises Alou

Felipe Alou was a three-time All-Star outfielder who played for several teams, including the San Francisco Giants and the Atlanta Braves. He was known for his ability to hit for both power and average. His son, Moises Alou, was a successful outfielder who played for several teams, including the Montreal Expos, the Chicago Cubs, and the San Francisco Giants. He was a six-time All-Star and won two Silver Slugger awards. This is only part of their baseball family. Felipe's brothers were Major Leaguers for 15 seasons, and cousin Jose Sosa had a short MLB career. Felipe and Moises played in MLB for 34 seasons and got over 4,200 hits, 500 homers, and 750 doubles.

5. Mel Stottlemyre and Todd Stottlemyre

Mel Stottlemyre was a five-time All-Star pitcher who played for the New York Yankees during the 1960s and 1970s. He was known for his consistency, intensity and ability to make his pitches count in big games. His son, Todd Stottlemyre, was also a pitcher who played for several teams, including the Toronto Blue Jays and the Arizona Diamondbacks. Unlike the other duos on this list, these two are pitchers. Mel was an All-Star five times during 11 seasons with the Yankees and ended his career with a 112 ERA+. Despite this, he was a better pitching coach, claiming World Series rings with the Yankees and the Mets. Mel's other son, Mel Jr., only played one season in the Majors, while Todd had a 14-year career and threw over 2,000 innings. Todd won championships with the 1992 and 1993 Blue Jays.

6. Sandy Alomar, Sandy Alomar Jr. and Roberto Alomar

Sandy Alomar had an incredible 15-year career, known for his dependable glove and 227 steals. His two sons experienced the joys of success beyond what their father had achieved. The younger son, Sandy, became a Rookie of the Year Award winner and six-time All-Star catcher. Alomar Jr. played for 20 seasons in the major leagues, mainly with the Cleveland Indians. He was a six-time All-

Star and won the Gold Glove Award for catchers in 1990, 1991, and 1992. Roberto turned into a Hall of Fame second baseman, making 12 All-Star teams from 1990 to 2001, getting 10 Gold Gloves, and winning two World Series with the '92-'93 Jays.

Imagine how special it was to these fathers and sons to play alongside (or against) each other, making memories to keep in their hearts forever. Cherish the time you spend with your parents, family, and friends; sure, it may not be on such a grand stage, but the memories you create together are special. A lifetime flies by faster than you think, and you'll be glad you made the effort to spend time with some of the most important people in your life.

Chapter 16
STEALS SECOND, GOES BACK TO STEAL FIRST

No, I didn't get the order wrong. The runner, Jean Segura, was on second base, for real. I'll break it down. If a runner has only one plate appearance, how can they steal the same base twice? Technically, it isn't possible but, thanks to one of the wildest plays you will ever see, this almost occurred on April 19, 2013, at Miller Park, where the Milwaukee Brewers hosted the Chicago Cubs.

Segura got on base with an infield hit to start the bottom of the eighth for the Brewers. After he stole second, the next batter, Ryan Braun, walked. Braun moved to second base when Segura was caught in a rundown between second and third base. After a bit more running around, Segura and Braun ended up on second base, and both players were tagged by the Cubs' third baseman.

The second base ump's ruling that Braun was out was correct, and Segura, the lead runner, had a right to the base as the runners were not required to advance at the time of the pitch. Valbuena then tagged out Segura, who was between the bases on the first base side and off the base, but there was no call. Since he thought he was out, Segura headed to the dugout. His first base coach pointed at first base (or was pointing toward first base), and, confused, Segura went to first. On his way, he was chased, but the Cubs' player couldn't make a play. A couple of pitches later, Segura attempted to steal second base but was called out.

Was Segura allowed to return to first? Can a runner run the bases in reverse? Did Segura abandon the base path? Did Segura get credited with the steal? Is there an error on the play? So many questions were thrown about! And everyone loves a bit of drama, don't they?

You be the judge if he did it intentionally or not? As long as it's not meant to confuse the defense or mock the game, Rule 7.08 says backward base running is actually allowed. Segura didn't seem like he was trying to mess with Chicago. He really seemed confused at the time, so the call stood. So, Segura had to steal second again, obviously. The fans sure hoped he would. And he did; he tried his best. But sadly, he was forced out.

Now, let's try this again. If a runner has only one plate appearance, can they steal the same base twice? Yes, it is possible, technically. Here, Lloyd Moseby steps up to help us out.

Once, in a game against the White Sox, he successfully stole second base, and the throw from the catcher went into center field.

The shortstop tricked Moseby by pretending the ball had popped up. Thinking he was about to be doubled off first, he ran back instead of staying on second base. Then, the center fielder threw to first but missed the base. Moseby made it back safely to second base on the error. The play ended with Moseby's hands flying up in disgust before he called for a timeout to, I'm sure, catch his breath (he was running full speed!).

There's not much to say here. It's important to stay focused and be aware of what's going on around you. It can save you time (and keep you from making costly mistakes). Life can be busy and we might feel we need to rush about, but staying present for that bit longer can make all the difference to the decisions you make.

Chapter 17
CHEATERS NEVER (REALLY) WIN

Please, though. Don't cheat!

The following goes into some unique tales that I hope you find silly, sad, and a little funny. You'll wonder how they didn't get caught sooner! What baffles me is why the home run counts. Why not take it back too? I'll explain.

On September 7, 1974, the Yankees' Graig Nettles hit a home run against the Detroit Tigers. Nettles' bat broke on a single—Bill Freeman froze, then quickly grabbed the six Superballs that spilled out.

Superballs are those tiny balls that have the best bounce because they are very "elasticky"—with the right amount of force. They can bounce back as high as two to two-and-a-half stories or more. Imagine the spring in a bat filled with six of these!

Nettles claims a fan gave him the bat, and he didn't realize it wasn't his regular bat. That excuse absolutely did not fly, and the broken-bat single was disallowed. Unfortunately, his earlier home run was left alone; that home run gave the Yankees the W.

How the bat got into the bat rack is also a mystery. If you guys solve it, let me know.

Listen to this one. On the mound, Whitey Ford coughed up the scoop about his gunky ball trick. It packed enough mud to build a dam, according to Ford. How did he get the gunk inside the ball? The ball was slit, providing the opening to hide the weighted surprise.

Supposedly, Ford used a roll-on deodorant container to hide the gunk in and carry it around. There were tales and jokes about his teammate Yogi Berra borrowing Ford's deodorant and having his arms glued to his sides! Ford eventually confessed to using the gunk against the Dodgers in the World Series. Not impressed, Ford!

Cheating when it's crunch time. I'm stuck between the 2017 Houston Astros and the 1951 New York Giants. I'll tell you why.

The Astros crushed the competition in the regular season, then took down the Yankees and Dodgers in a seven-game series to take the 2017 crown, winning 8 out of 9 postseason games at home.

While the Astros were exposed for cheating two years after their scam, the Giants'—who lost the World Series to the Yankees in six games—their secret was safe for five decades until reporter Joshua Prager revealed it. His report also discusses the history of the tricks used to illegally steal the opposing catcher's signals.

The first instance happened in 1898 or 1899 with the Philadelphia Phillies using a pair of opera glasses or hiding someone behind the center field wall. The New York Highlanders used the spy behind the center field wall trick in 1909, and so did the Chicago Cubs in 1946.

The Giants' path to "steal" glory started with a heart-warming and fantastic story about their race toward the National League pennant; it was the origin story of the most famous home run in baseball history: the "Shot Heard Round the World."

Both teams had someone in center field to spy on the other catcher and transmit their signals to the batter. The Astros had a camera in center field sending a live feed to the dugout. The Giants had a coach with a small telescope watching the bullpen, and he'd sound the buzzer to let the players know the next pitch or a random ball would be used as the signal. The Astros got their message across with a bang of a trash can.

On July 19, 1951, with the season all but lost, the Giants manager called a meeting to explain the new scheme. With the season nearly ending, the Giants were tied atop the standings. Off to the playoffs, they go to face the Dodgers.

We'll jump right to the bottom of the ninth inning of the last game of that playoff series. The Dodgers were up 4-1. The Giants slowly start crawling back into the game. Third baseman Bobby Thomson walks up to the plate with two runners on. He knocks an 0-1 fastball from Ralph Branca over the left field wall, unleashing a frenzy in New York that day and the epic call by radio broadcaster Russ Hodges: "The Giants win the pennant! The Giants win the pennant! The Giants win the pennant!"

Now, that's no baseball. Both stories are pretty bad, and sad, because they've ruined historical moments. Anyway, it's easy to cheat and the truth always comes out in the end, and I'm sure the cheaters would be full of regret. So remember to play fair. And enjoy the wonderful feeling of winning for real.

Chapter 18
BEAUTIFUL STEALS

Let's talk about Rickey Henderson. Gosh, the way that man could take your joy with a well-timed steal, and you just knew once he had second base that he would end up scoring!

Rickey Henderson holds the all-time MLB career stolen base record with 1,406 steals, and he is the only player to reach 1,000 stolen bases. Lou Brock ranks second on the all-time stolen base list with 938, followed by Billy Hamilton (exact career steals numbers vary by source) in third place before Ty Cobb, Tim Raines, Vince Coleman, Arlie Latham, Eddie Collins, Max Carey, and Honus Wagner, all of whom have stolen at least 700 bases. Coleman is the leader for retired players not in the Hall of Fame.

Brock held the career stolen base record from 1977 to 1991 before being surpassed by Henderson. Hamilton had the record for 81 years from 1897 to 1977, while Latham held the record from 1887 to 1896 and was the first player to collect 300 career stolen bases.

Henderson could steal an incredible number of bases, showing off his impressive speed and knowledge of the game. Henderson's stolen base record results from when he was in his prime. Stealing bases wasn't cool after Babe Ruth made the home run popular in the 1920s; but between 1970 to 1990, stealing was popular again!

Funny how things change. What also boosted numbers is that back then, walks, singles, and hit-by-pitches accounted for 78 to 81 percent of all on-base occurrences. However, this is the unavoidable result of different perspectives regarding the risks and rewards of stolen bases.

Would you believe the Oakland A's hated stealing so much that they had a rule? All things considered, that rule did what it was supposed to. If you make it, great! If you failed at the steal attempt, you'd be in a ton of trouble.

Henderson's got an impressive record, but he's also got the all-time lead for times caught stealing in both MLB and the AL.

Henderson was caught stealing 335 times throughout his career, a record 293 of those in the American League. And during his entire time in the National League, Lou Brock was caught stealing 307 times.

Henderson and Brock also hold the records for most times caught stealing in a single season in their respective leagues. Henderson got thrown out 42 times in 1982 and broke the post-1900 (20th-century era) record with 130 steals that year. Brock got caught stealing 33 times in 1974, the year he broke the NL record for steals with 118. Aggressive baserunning helped Henderson and Brock set records.

There's a few things to think about here. Like the fine line between passion and aggression. Sometimes it's hard to know when you're going too far. Simply put, your passion is the cause—think about your goal or a dream you're working toward. Likeminded people will notice this and will be attracted to you. Aggression is more selfish;

it can push people away from you as they won't be able to see your goals or your passion, because your negativity is driving them away. Again, I think you guys can walk the fine line between being super passionate and being fair and a sportsman.

Chapter 19
PITCHING DUELS

Sandy Koufax was known for his dominant pitching performances throughout his career. Still, his most famous pitching duel came in Game 7 of the 1965 World Series against the Minnesota Twins.

Koufax had already pitched a complete game shutout in Game 5 of the series, but Game 7 would be even more impressive. Facing the Twins' ace pitcher, Jim Kaat, Koufax took the mound for the Dodgers on just two days' rest. Not bad!

The game was scoreless through the first three innings, but Koufax gave up a solo home run to Twins' slugger Harmon Killebrew in the top of the fourth. The Dodgers tied it up in the fifth, but Koufax was in trouble in the sixth with runners on second and third. Koufax dug deep and got the three strikeouts. He then retired the side in the seventh and eighth innings, setting the stage for one of the most memorable moments in World Series history.

In the bottom of the eighth inning, Dodgers catcher John Roseboro hit a ground ball to Twins' third baseman Rich Rollins, who threw wildly to first base. The ball got away, and Dodgers runner Jim Lefebvre rounded third and headed for home. Twins' center fielder Joe Nossek fielded the ball and threw to the plate, where Roseboro was waiting to tag Lefebvre out.

The play at the plate was close, and Lefebvre appeared to slide in safely, but the home plate umpire called him out. The Dodgers argued the call vehemently, but Koufax calmly took the mound for the top of the ninth inning, determined to close out the game.

He retired the first two batters he faced. Then he got the final out on a fly ball to left field, securing a 2-0 victory for the Dodgers and their third World Series championship in five years.

Koufax's performance in the game was nothing short of heroic. He pitched a complete game shutout on two days' rest, allowing only three hits and striking out ten batters. A remarkable display of pitching skill and mental toughness cemented Koufax's place as one of the greatest pitchers ever.

Next stop, another legendary series. It's 1995, and so far, this World Series duel between Smoltz and Pettitte was remarkable. The Braves had won the World Series against the Yankees two years ago. The Yankees wanted revenge, setting the stage for a legendary showdown. The pressure was on for both pitchers to deliver in the decisive Game 5.

The game was a pitcher's duel from start to finish. Smoltz struck out eight batters and allowed just two hits and no runs over eight innings. At the same time, Pettitte matched him almost pitch for pitch, striking out five batters and allowing just four hits and one run over seven and a third innings.

The game's only run came in the top of the fourth inning when Braves first baseman Fred McGriff hit a solo home run off Pettitte. It was a tense moment for the Yankees, who struggled to get anything going against Smoltz's dominant pitching!

The game remained 1-0 in favor of the Braves until the top of the ninth inning when the Yankees mounted a rally against Braves' closer Mark Wohlers. With runners on first and second and two outs, Yankees pinch hitter Jim Leyritz hit a dramatic three-run home run to give the Yankees the lead.

The Braves could not answer in the bottom of the ninth, and the Yankees secured a thrilling 4-1 victory to take a 3-2 lead in the series.

The game was remarkable not only for its high stakes and intense rivalry but also for the exceptional pitching performances of Smoltz and Pettitte. Both pitchers showed incredible poise and skill under pressure. Their duel will go down as one of the greatest in World Series history.

I wonder how you manage stressful or tense situations? Do you handle them okay? It takes practice, but keeping calm helps keep your mind clear to make better decisions. It lets you act more quickly under pressure, allows you to into your instincts, use your reasoning skills and think clearly, act quickly, and do what needs to be done! So keep cool, guys! And you know what? The more you work on keeping calm, the easier it gets.

Chapter 20
GREATEST PITCHERS

Time to round out the field by highlighting the greatest pitcher(s) ever. I think pitchers and (excellent stealing) baserunners are the best things about baseball. What about you? What do you love the most?

I know I spoke about steals earlier, and yes, the last story was about pitching duels.

But I had to talk about pitchers again.

It's the best way to end our journey.

Think about it.

The game wouldn't be the game it is without the command, the unique stances, shaking off the calls, sinkers, sliders, the mastery of finding the right spot up and in, the strikes, balks, and seriously, the ceremonial pitches that don't make it to the plate. This is where the magic resides. Here are three of the greatest pitchers, according to me. Who are your favorite pitchers?

Randy Johnson, affectionately known as "The Big Unit," is one of the most dominant pitchers to ever take the mound. Johnson played for six teams during his career. He is best known for his time with the Seattle Mariners and the Arizona Diamondbacks. During his career, Johnson won 303 games, recorded 4,875 strikeouts, and had an ERA of 3.29. His best season came in 2002, when he won 24 games, had a 2.32 ERA, and struck out an incredible 334 batters. Johnson was famous for his height, competitive nature, and slider, which confused hitters. Johnson was inducted into the Hall of Fame in 2015.

Another all-time great pitcher is Nolan Ryan. Ryan played for four teams during his career, but he is best known for his time with the Houston Astros and the Texas Rangers. During his career, Ryan won 324 games, recorded 5,714 strikeouts, and had an ERA of 3.19. His best season came in 1973, when he won 21 games, had a 2.87 ERA, and struck out an incredible 383 batters. Ryan's fastball was over 100 mph and he played until he was 46 years—and was inducted into the Hall of Fame in 1999.

Pedro Martinez was a smaller pitcher than Ryan and Johnson but no less dominant! Martinez had a unique blend of pitches, including a fastball, changeup, and curveball. He played for 18 seasons, pitching for the Los Angeles Dodgers, Montreal Expos, Boston Red Sox, New York Mets, and Philadelphia Phillies. Martinez won three Cy Young Awards and finished his career with 3,154 strikeouts. He was known for his fiery competitiveness and ability to outthink his opponents on the mound.

Together, Ryan, Johnson, and Martinez represent some of the greatest pitchers in baseball history. Their dominance on the mound was unmatched, and their legacies continue to inspire young players today.

I truly hope all of these stories have inspired you to not necessarily

take up baseball, but fully jump in something you're passionate about! Give it your all. Be yourself. Think how unique all of these players are. Their uniqueness was their gift and what people still read about today. And girls, think of Jackie, nothing held her back from doing what she loved, with baseball, and the rest of her life.

So, Seize the day! (that's an old Roman proverb.) We often feel a little unsure of going for our dreams, but you have nothing to lose, guys. Try different things, have a go, and most of all, have fun. You'll be surprised at the results!

References

A pigeon gave its life to improve Dion James'... - UPI Archives. (1987, April 12). UPI. https://www.upi.com/Archives/1987/04/12/A-pigeon-gave-its-life-to-improve-Dion-James/9271545198400/

Acocella, N. (n.d.). ESPN.com - CLASSIC - SportsCentury biography of Bill Veeck. Www.espn.com. Retrieved April 9, 2023, from http://www.espn.com/classic/veeckbill000816.html#:~:text=ESPN.com%20%2D%20CLASSIC%20%2D%20SportsCentury%20biography%20of%20Bill%20Veeck&text=Just%20as%20he%20predicted%2C%20Bill

Benvie, C. (2012, January 10). Is Pedro Martinez the Greatest MLB Pitcher of All Time? Bleacher Report. https://bleacherreport.com/articles/1018983-pedro-martinez-is-he-the-greatest-pitcher-of-all-time

Big League Stew. (2012, September 30). Michael Morse repeats grand slam swing after overturned call re-starts game (Video). Yahoo Sports. https://sports.yahoo.com/blogs/big-league-stew/michael-morse-repeats-grand-slam-swing-overturned-call-042433569--mlb.html

Castrovince, A. (2022, December 26). The "Curse of the Bambino," explained. MLB.com. https://www.mlb.com/news/curse-of-the-bambino

Chichester, R. (2016, October 24). Game Five of the 1996 World Series was a pitchers' duel for the ages. Pinstripe Alley. https://www.pinstripealley.com/2016/10/24/13371592/yankees-history-1996-world-series-andy-pettitte-john-smoltz-braves

Chiusano, S. (2022, September 29). Willie Mays always knew he'd make The Catch. MLB.com. https://www.mlb.com/news/willie-mays-the-catch

Dakers, T. (2021, August 4). Today in Blue Jays history: Dave Winfield kills a seagull. Bluebird Banter. https://www.bluebirdbanter.com/2021/8/4/22609567/

today-in-blue-jays-history-dave-winfield-kills-a-seagull

ESPN.com - Page2 - Biggest cheaters in baseball. (n.d.). Www.espn.com. Retrieved April 19, 2023, from https://www.espn.com/page2/s/list/cheaters/ballplayers.html

Ferguson, R. (2015, September 17). Remembering Sadaharu Oh, Japan's home run king. The Guardian. https://www.theguardian.com/sport/2015/sep/17/baseball-sadaharu-oh-japans-home-run-king

Ghiroli, B. (2023, March 27). How many bases would Rickey Henderson steal under MLB's new rules? We asked him. The Athletic. https://theathletic.com/4349809/2023/03/27/rickey-henderson-stolen-bases-mlb/

Hanlon, J. (1965, June 21). QUEEN LIZZIE PLAYS FIRST BASE. Vault.SI.com. https://vault.si.com/vault/1965/06/21/queen-lizzie-plays-first-base

Hockensmith, R. (2021, August 24). The incredible story of the MLB pitcher who survived a lightning strike to finish a game. ESPN.com. https://www.espn.com/mlb/story/_/id/32061845/the-incredible-story-mlb-pitcher-survived-lightning-strike-finish-game

Huber, Mike. (n.d.). July 3, 1966: Braves pitcher Tony Cloninger clouts two grand slams – Society for American Baseball Research. SABR. Retrieved April 18, 2023, from https://sabr.org/gamesproj/game/july-3-1966-braves-pitcher-tony-cloninger-clouts-two-grand-slams/

Hunter, I. (2010, May 7). Flashback Friday: Lloyd Moseby steals second base twice in one play. Blue Jay Hunter. http://bluejayhunter.com/2010/05/acid-flashback-friday-lloyd-moseby.html

Jackman, T. (2020, February 13). Baseball's cheating history includes its most famous home run, the "Shot Heard 'Round the World'. Washington Post. https://www.washingtonpost.com/history/2020/02/13/giants-cheating-home-run-1951/

Jugs. (2018, August 28). The Sports Illustrated Jinx. Jugs Sports. https://jugssports.com/the-sports-illustrated-jinx/

King, Norm. (n.d.). October 14, 1965: Koufax has nothing to atone for in Game 7 masterpiece – Society for American Baseball Research. SABR. Retrieved April 19, 2023, from https://sabr.org/gamesproj/game/october-14-1965-koufax-has-nothing-to-atone-for-in-game-seven-masterpiece/

Lehman, J. (2014, April 24). Great moments in baseball cheaters' history. New York Post. https://nypost.com/2014/04/24/great-moments-in-baseball-cheaters/

List of top 500 Major League Baseball home run hitters. (n.d.). Baseball Wiki. Retrieved April 18, 2023, from https://baseball.fandom.com/wiki/List_of_top_500_Major_League_Baseball_home_run_hitters

Miller, M. (2011, November 11). 50 of the Funniest Moments in Baseball History. Bleacher Report. https://bleacherreport.com/articles/924871-50-of-the-funniest-moments-in-baseball-history

Miller, S. (2015, January 6). Inside Randy Johnson's Transformation from Awkward Enigma to "The Big Unit." Bleacher Report. https://bleacherreport.com/articles/2320316-inside-randy-johnsons-transformation-from-awkward-enigma-to-the-big-unit

Monagan, M. (2022, February 2). How did a mascot get ejected from a game? MLB.com. https://www.mlb.com/news/mascot-gets-ejected-from-game

Morosi, J. P. (2022, September 13). It's not just Judge: Slugger chasing HR record an ocean away. MLB.com. https://www.mlb.com/news/munetaka-murakami-nearing-home-run-record-in-japan

Osborne, Chad. (n.d.). August 24, 1919: Ray Caldwell struck by lightning, sparks Indians to win – Society for American Baseball Research. SABR. Retrieved April 17, 2023, from https://sabr.org/gamesproj/game/august-24-1919-ray-caldwell-struck-by-lightning-sparks-indians-to-win/

Pizzi, V. (2010, February 11). The Home Run King You Don't Kn-Oh. Bleacher Report. https://bleacherreport.com/articles/343793-the-home-run-king-you-dont-kn-oh

Pop Fly Turns To Double When Ball Hits Bird. (1987, April 12). AP NEWS. https://apnews.com/article/7eccb1ea56330a11565bdd576e409399

Posnanski, J. (2017, February 10). SI prediction gave Cleveland false hope in '87. MLB.com. https://www.mlb.com/news/sports-illustrated-gave-87-indians-false-hope-c215708352

Rainey, Chris. (n.d.). April 8, 1993: Baerga hits two homers in one inning – Society for American Baseball Research. SABR. Retrieved April 18, 2023, from https://sabr.org/gamesproj/game/april-8-1993-baerga-hits-two-homers-in-one-inning/

Randhawa, M. (2022a, April 26). "Nobody does that!" Mitchell's catch still stuns. MLB.com. https://www.mlb.com/news/kevin-mitchell-barehanded-catch

Randhawa, M. (2022b, December 24). Will anyone ever threaten this Rickey record? MLB.com. https://www.mlb.com/news/rickey-henderson-sets-steals-record-in-1982

Readmikenow. (2022, May 18). Jackie Mitchell: The Woman Who Struck Out Babe Ruth and Lou Gehrig. HowTheyPlay. https://howtheyplay.com/team-sports/Jackie-Mitchell-was-the-only-professional-Female-Baseball-player-to-Strike-Out-Babe-Ruth-and-then-Lou-Gehrig

Reuter, J. (2012, November 1). The 25 Greatest World Series Pitcher's Duels of All Time. Bleacher Report. https://bleacherreport.com/articles/1391753-the-25-greatest-world-series-pitchers-duels-of-all-time

Roberts, J. (2021, October 11). The Eccentric Life of Rube Waddell. Odd Sports Stories. https://oddsportsstories.com/2021/10/11/the-eccentric-life-of-rube-waddell/#:~:text=He%20played%20on%20numerous%20teams

Rymer, Z. D. (n.d.). It's Time to Add Rickey Henderson's Stolen Bases to MLB's Unbreakable Records. Bleacher Report. Retrieved April 19, 2023, from https://bleacherreport.com/articles/2887279-its-time-to-add-rickey-hendersons-stolen-bases-to-mlbs-unbreakable-records#:~:text=That%20Henderson%20was%20able%20to

Rymer, Z. D. (2014, August 22). Dissecting Nolan Ryan's One-of-a-Kind Legacy, 25 Years After 5,000th Strikeout. Bleacher Report. https://bleacherreport.com/articles/2171101-dissecting-nolan-ryans-one-of-a-kind-legacy-25-years-after-5000th-strikeout

Simon, A. (2012, June 19). The greatest father-son duos in MLB history. MLB.com. https://www.mlb.com/news/greatest-father-son-duos-in-mlb-history-c50711176

Smith Muniz, C. (2018, April 25). Carlos Baerga's Cleveland memories. La Vida Baseball. https://www.lavidabaseball.com/carlos-baerga-puerto-rico/

Steven A. King. (2013). The Strangest Month in the Strange Career of Rube Waddell – Society for American Baseball Research. SABR.org. https://sabr.org/journal/article/the-strangest-month-in-the-strange-career-of-rube-waddell/

Team, I. S. E. (2022, October 8). The 10 Best MLB Base Stealers in History | Got the Green Light. Imagine Sports. https://imaginesports.com/news/best-mlb-base-stealers

Townsend, M. (2013, April 20). Jean Segura steals second, then steals first in bizarre baserunning adventure (video). Yahoo Sports. http://ca.sports.yahoo.com/blogs/mlb-big-league-stew/jean-segura-steals-second-then-steals-first-bizarre-103642855--mlb.html

Tuiskula, L. (2020, March 8). Warren, RI Native Lizzie Murphy: The. MiLB.com. https://www.milb.com/news/lizzie-murphy

Turnquist, R. (n.d.). Bill Veeck, Eddie Gaedel and the Birth of Legend | Baseball Hall of Fame. Baseballhall.org. Retrieved April 9, 2023, from https://baseballhall.org/discover-more/stories/inside-pitch/bill-veeck-eddie-gaedel-the-birth-of-a-legend

USATODAY. (2012, September). Nationals' Michael Morse hits invisible home run. USA TODAY. https://www.usatoday.com/story/gameon/2012/09/29/nationals-michael-morse-hits-invisible-home-run/1603627/

Welsh, C. (2020, June 3). That Time Jean Segura Stole 1B, Really! Baseball Rules Academy. https://baseballrulesacademy.com/that-time-jean-segura-stole-1b-really/#:~:text=If%20he%20was%20tagged%20between

Youngson, S. (2022, May 26). The Top Ten Pitchers of All-Time. Pitcher List. https://www.pitcherlist.com/the-top-ten-pitchers-of-all-time/

Zant, J. (2007, October 4). The Catch Heard 'Round the World. The Santa Barbara Independent. https://www.independent.com/2007/10/04/catch-heard-round-world/

www.ingramcontent.com/pod-product-compliance
Lightning Source LLC
Chambersburg PA
CBHW070306120526
44590CB00017B/2577